# SAVAGE SONNETS
# Finding Freedom Through Poetry

# Zechariah N. Frame, PhD

**SAVAGE SONNETS
Finding Freedom Through Poetry**

FICTION4ALL

A FICTION4ALL PAPERBACK

© *Copyright 2022*
*Zechariah N. Frame, PhD*

The right of Zechariah N. Frame, PhD to be identified as author of this work has been asserted in accordance with the Copyright, Designs and Patents Act 1988

**All Rights Reserved**

No reproduction, copy or transmission of the publication may be made without written permission.

No paragraph of this publication may be reproduced, Copied or transmitted save with the written permission of the publisher, or in accordance with the provisions of the Copyright Act 1956 (as amended).

Any person who does any unauthorised act in relation to this publication may be liable to criminal prosecution and civil claims for damages.

ISBN: 978 1 78695 766 5

Published by
Fiction4All

This Edition Published 2022

## ACKNOWLEDGEMENTS

There are many people in my life who inspired this collection of poetry. My husband, partner, and best friend, Alex, has been with me every step of the way as we navigate the neurologically uncertain waters of multiple sclerosis. He has picked me up, literally and figuratively, consistently and without fail since the beginning of this affliction. I would struggle to be all that I can be without him. Even when we have considerable challenges to overcome daily, we still enjoy the things life has to offer together.

I'd like to offer a special thank you to my illustrators, my sister, Brittani, and former English student, Shannon, for working to provide a visual representation to the emotional chaos I have put into poetry. Adding illustrations has been an adventure in itself. I am thankful that these women worked with me and used the details to really give life to this project.

Erika has been a consistent factor in my life since high school. Thank you for being the mirror you are and providing the insights you do. We have done some of our best growth together. There are always layers to the lessons.

Trevor Wicken, the MS Gym, the MOC, and the fantastic community of MS warrior athletes who continue to work on and improve the programs and the quality of people's lives through their support, love, coaching, guidance and sacrifice.

Thank you, Norm, for giving me an opportunity to share my experience with the world. We never know how far our influence reaches, or where it stops.

No doubt about it, my mom was always my biggest fan. Her passing has left a hole in my heart that no amount of poetry can fill. Rest in peace. Thank you for choosing to give me life.

Finally, my grandmother. I have a lot in common with my grandmother, and as I get older, it becomes more obvious. She was a writer of beautiful poems and some aspects of feeling confined were echoed in her poetry. Thank you, MaMa, for passing your intuitive gifts and way with words down to me.

Zechariah N. Frame

# ILLUSTRATION CREDITS

**Brittani Frame** for the illustrations for sonnets number one, two, three, four, five, six, seven, eight, 11, 12, 14, 17, 18, 19, 20, 21, 22, 23, 26, 27, 30, 31, 32, 34, 36, 40, 46, 50, 55, 57, 59, 60, 61, 62, 63, 65, 66, 67, and 68 and 70.

**Shannon Packer** for the illustrations for sonnets number nine, 10, 13, 15, 16, 24, 25, 28, 29, 33, 35, 37, 38, 39, 41, 42, 43, 44, 45, 47, 48, 49, 51, 52, 53, 54 , 56, 58, 64, 69, 70 and 71.

Sonnet number 70 also contains artwork from both illustrators.

"Now and Then" was illustrated primarily by Shannon Packer, however, the bonnet and the rose at the base of the tree were illustrated by Brittani Frame.

# Savage Sonnets

## PREFACE

Living with multiple sclerosis for 17 years has certainly had its challenges. There are many days I wish I could go for a run to clear my head, or sit in a challenging yoga position to contemplate my struggles... but unfortunately, my disease has progressed in such a way that these physical outlets are not options for me. So what is a person supposed to do to process their emotional energy?

Sure, crying helps. But it only goes so far.

As a certified life coach, educator, and trauma survivor, I know that keeping it buried will have negative long-term effects. Lashing out at others is a pretty negative practice as well. Punching bags are not much of a thing and water activities don't typically pan out for wheelchair users. Again, what are my options?

I write.

I have written many letters that I will never send. It's therapeutic. Over time, I have learned that it is more important for me to write the letter and get it out of my system than it is for any person to receive it. As above, so below. When I hold on to an energy that I have been physically unable to process, I have physical symptoms. Maybe I am sick to my stomach, maybe I have a headache, maybe I develop a sore throat or a cough... my body has taught me through countless examples that if I do not process the energy, it will make me sick.

These sonnets are a reflection of emotions or feelings that I was unable to process in the moment of writing for whatever reason. Some of the sonnets capture progression of disability and provide an image to my ever-fading physical ability. Things like grooming, dressing, feeling forgotten by loved ones, marital challenges, physical challenges... Some of these themes are common even for the able-bodied, but with the additional strain of a handicap, simple tasks are anything but simple-leaving the soul to yearn for an escape. Just like life, it isn't all bad. There are humorous and lighthearted poems, as well as poems of love, celebration, birthdays and anniversaries.

They say not to judge a book by its cover, but the cover of this book does a pretty good job capturing the emotion between the pages. An overturned wheelchair signals a cry for help, but it also represents leaving the shell behind and elevating to a higher perspective.

The illustrations serve as a supplement to the written word. There is symbolism in the art. The artistic styles vary from classroom sketches to competition pieces. But that's life, isn't it? Sometimes life works out in all of the perfect ways. Sometimes it just doesn't. Sometimes we make sketches just to pass the time. And sometimes we are really invested.

The poetry herein is freeing. The emotions that sparked the writing were fleeting moments that felt confining, isolating, celebratory, funny, overwhelming, suffocating and painful. By taking the energy of the negative emotions and channeling them into digestible poems, I have given myself wings to fly to a perspective where things seem small. —Pain transmuted into freedom!

## Savage Sonnets

Zechariah N. Frame

# Sonnet No. 1

Sometimes I find myself filled with emotion,
And many are a struggle to express.
Varied are the tides and deep like an ocean,
All are suffocating- leading to stress.
Grief, regret, love, joy and pain
Expressed through poetry and writing.
Since holding it in shows no real gain,
Oh and I certainly prefer it over fighting.
Now lots of these words are poignant and raw,
Not with any intent of malice-
Even the hits that impact the jaw,
Teach blistered lessons for time to callous.
Savage sonnets are a deep expression of me,
… and expressing it so allows me to be free.

## Sonnet No. 2

When I look at myself,
I see a ripped fabric.
A blanket on a shelf,
Who's purpose's gone static.
I was once full of life,
With drive, purpose and care.
But now it's just strife.
And I don't belong anywhere.
My blanket is faded.
Too many times washed cold.
My threads are now jaded.
My colors aren't bold.
When will He see that I am a gift?
When should I quit waiting for a shift?

Zechariah N. Frame

## Sonnet No. 3

When I see how far I have come
It's hard to keep moving on.
This would be too much for some.
I crave to graze a greener lawn.
The lessons of life have made me strong
But have also hurt my soul.
I wish to halt the pain, "so long."
For the losses make it hard to feel whole.
To process the pain, I take to the pen,
Only I can process what I feel.
The angst within, between seven and 10,
I write so that I can heal.
The poetry captures things I need to say;
But most things can be said another way.

## Sonnet No. 4

Luck doesn't mean anything.
It's all about perspective;
Just because One doesn't sing,
Doesn't mean One's not protective.
You win the bet, you feel the luck,
Winning can make us feel good.
But when you are the guy who lost all his fucks,
You wish that's not where you stood.
Now is a special moment,
For it's the only moment we're gift.
Luck can happen, at least condone it,
Momentarily, release and let stress sift.
Life isn't about being raped by fate.
It's about opening your heart and letting go of hate.

Zechariah N. Frame

# Sonnet No. 5

I have you on a hydraulic pedestal,
To compensate for the weather.
Other times you seem premenstrual,
Flipping tables at the drop of a feather-
I remind you of your excellence;
Encourage, support and believe in you.
But you view me through eyes of petulance,
Even if it's only a hue.
As a result of my defense,
I send the platform sky high.
Hyperbolically beyond what makes sense,
And with apprehension, I sigh.
I am consciously increasing the space.
Soon, I won't see your face.

## Sonnet No. 6: The Things You Do

Simply making a list of the things you do,
Would be an injustice to language and intent.
The steps you travel are walked by few,
No one knows how your energy is spent.
It's more than just the tasks mundane,
You pick up a lot of slack.
The tasks are harder with holes in the brain,
As time moves on, the adversities stack.
More than anything this is an acknowledgment,
I don't mean to make things hard.
You are a gift, from heaven sent,
Knowing just where to hide that MS card.
Sometimes I feel like a caged bird.
Other times I feel like a caged turd.

Zechariah N. Frame

## Sonnet No. 7

When we wed, I was never a trophy wife.
At least not in a physical sense.
I never feel you're proud of our life-
Social events including me? Wince.
Heaven is a place much different from this-
Yes, six packs, men and gratuitous nudity.
It's a place begging for more than a kiss,
-excluding tungsten, wheels and me.
Weddings, hikes, and gatherings galore;
These are things to share with a spouse.
But the empty acknowledgment leaves me wanting more,
It's easier to leave it at the house.
When it's me, why do you feel so ashamed?
Be proud of my strength. I need not blamed.

## Sonnet No 8 - I Wanna Die

Not a physical death, yet, death in a sense.
I don't even know what that means.
Out of the blue, we get so tense,
I can only imagine your brain scenes.
The timing is wrong.
Dropping bombs like flower girls spread petals.
I'm sorry if my recovery is long.
The bars around my heart are upgraded metals.
I poke fun not at the symptoms of our state.
But inquire for my own sanity,
Why Tourette's when takin' the 'bate?
Is it always a good time for profanity?
No, I didn't even turn my head,
Does it matter if you'd rather be dead?

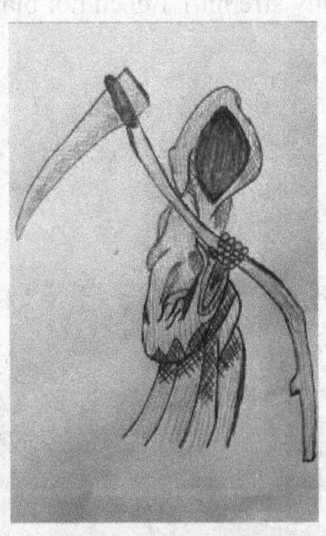

Zechariah N. Frame

## Sonnet No 9

And then he asked, then why do you stay?
An inquiry that surprisingly left me puzzled.
I paused. Forever brief. Dumb what to say.
All at once, my emotions are muzzled.
I love you more than I can love myself.
Which is silly to see it in writing.
I don't always feel like a blanket on the shelf.
But please, let us work on the timing.
A fear of lost time, of lessons unlearned...
The chill of an empty bed...
Perception of loss, or worse, being burned...
A sea of guilt that's thick in my head.
Is it love or fear that attracts me to you?
Or is it my chronic desire to feel ever blue?

## Sonnet No. 10

20 years of school
To learn to be a teacher-
At the time was cool
But now I am a preacher.
The word of God is fine,
As long as it's High Vibration.
Have doubt? Ask for a sign.
It even works on vacation.
Ask while keeping your eyes open wide:
You can't see if they are closed.
Take caution, neon signs are hard to hide.
And will leave you feeling exposed.
Signs are vital for our evergrowing being
But they can be rough before they are freeing.

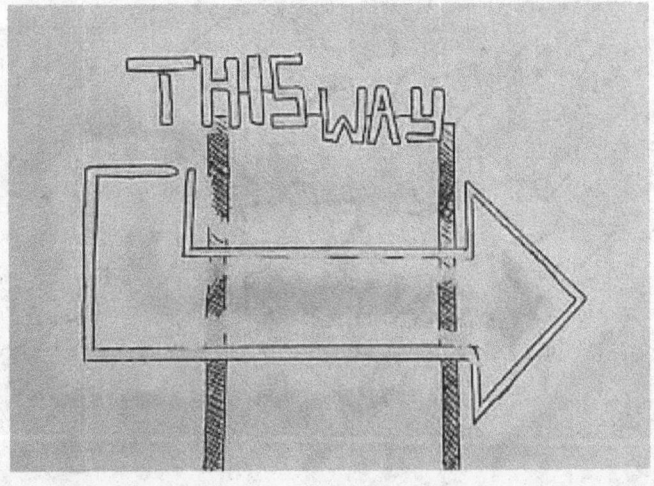

Zechariah N. Frame

## Sonnet No. 11

Your spirit is dead,
You don't even care.
Make me sad before bed,
Like the pain is fair.
This is my towel, I'm throwing it in.
Science can't inspire Self improvement.
Sub-atomic or Divine. It is all Sin.
-That still doesn't tell us where the soul went.
It doesn't matter if you resist the Spirit pill.
Everyone takes it when it's time.
It's not likely to affect your will,
But happiness is not a crime.
I obviously have no respect-
Because I try harder each time you reject.

## Sonnet No. 12

Are you still pissed at me?
-but with genuine quizzical glance.
-With guilt enough to know and see
My happiness isn't happenstance.
If I'm pissed about anything-
It's feeling taken for granted,
-Resisting when positive vibes sing.
... negated rivers persistently chanted.
I could be pissed for things out of my control.
And for some of them, I am. Yes.
I accept what is mine, the all, the whole.
I sleep well; I know I do my best.
No, I'm not pissed at you.
I want you to see you the way I do.

Zechariah N. Frame

## Sonnet No. 13

Gotta get a head start on the week's end,
Of the arguments we get to engage.
With preferences neither can let bend.
Bend. Bend. Breaking. Broke. Rage.
Who's fault is it this time?
Who's casting stones in a glass house?
For the guilty is accused the same crime-
And who is right? Correct. The spouse.
We can choose not to dance,
Or be in different ball rooms.
But I think we could jive if we gave it a chance.
Let us dance outside of tombs.
The weekend can be a good choice.
But we have to hear each other's voice.

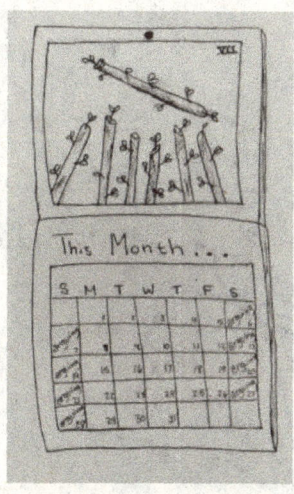

## Sonnet No. 14

Now I lay in bed to sleep,
Spurts of romance in my mind.
Internal. Sudden- ...urges to weep.
Is that a love of the right kind?
Now I wake in dreams Untold,
A Vision of marital bliss.
-A Sight to learn, and love to be bold.
Does it always feel like a bris?
Now I see with Clarity's hindsight,
Each stance has plenty to fault.
Fueled by love, lust, loyalty and might-
Should that be locked in a vault?
Love is simple arithmetic.
Life is an elaborate magic trick.

Zechariah N. Frame

# Sonnet No. 15

Unforgivable words
pierce more than the heart;
They spoil the soul like rotten cheese curds,
And that's where regret gets its start.
A shock to the motherboard;
Inspiring faulty connections-
Checking in to the mental ward-
Aspiring false corrections.
Simple, yet savvy, Soothsayers say
Spoken words shan't be unsaid.
Hateful words have a high price to pay:
Leading to emotional poverty and dread.
The words of choice feel charged and mean.
But unforgivable words make us unclean.

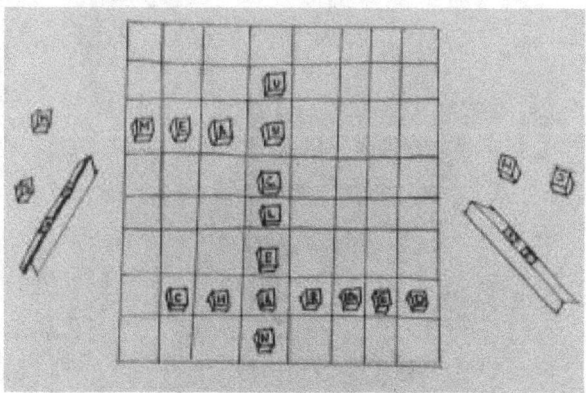

# Sonnet No. 16

There was an interesting epiphany,
That came out of the blue.
But the realization was about me-
As that's how my epiphanies do.
I have a negative trend of unfortunate size;
It's a troubling form of self-talk.
It's my crippling bad habit to personalize;
And feel guilty for not being able to walk.
Knowing this bad babble I have of myself,
Is a reminder that there's still work to do,
I should read the books I have on the shelf,
And some work with self-esteem'd help, too.
It's hard to know what it is we need to know.
And knowing the unknown is needed to grow.

Zechariah N. Frame

## Sonnet No. 17

I hate when words hurt,
-I loathe so much pain.
And these words may be curt;
But the pain's in the brain.
Words whispered loud and aghast,
Words spoken assertive and strong.
Words explosive; a dynamite blast,
Words lose air only after so long.
Where do we go when words fall short?
Where does communication shift?
Where is the export as Ship leaves port?
Where go the sands in a divided rift?
The perfect combo of subjects and words,
Fall short of Enlightenment if we feel like wounded birds.

## Sonnet No. 18

Opportunity to sustain should not be a pain.
Confection-y chocolate or a banana?
The answer is simple to avoid weight gain,
But concentrated sugar is sweet stamina.
Beloved banana, yellow and bright.
Dear fruit who is perfectly peeling.
I know your taste will bring fruity delight.
And nothing can replace the natural feeling.
Nuggets of crack you could call chocolate,
Found coated on dozens of raisins-
Make the sugar high fly higher than an auklet.
And with crack, you'll always have cravin's.
It's challenging because I ought to choose.
But if I choose both… I simply can't lose.

Zechariah N. Frame

# Sonnet No. 19

I approve of myself.
Whether others do or not.
I choose to put sad thoughts on the shelf.
They really don't need to be bought.
For me, I have unconditional love.
That flows like streams of forgiveness.
A kind acceptance. No need to shove.
The past is no longer my business.
Silence stings.
But not today.
I have wings.
I love myself anyway.
I accept myself all the time.
Even when things seem out of line.

## Sonnet No. 20

I want to scale the mountains.
But the mountains shan't be touched.
The rocks are populated with demons;
They challenge my climbing and such.
The Hotel Fabrics fancy the force
with which I wish to travel...
It's decided. Bland is the course!
Tortured dreams scattered on gravel.
Mt. Evans: Terrifyingly tall,
Rocky roads, and oxygen thin...
Falling short once, I still hear your call.
I'm foolish for fighting fate again.
Sometimes the prize in the victory
comes out of learning from the history.

Zechariah N. Frame

# Sonnet No. 21

I want attention,
I need it now.
Some conversation;
Some way, some how.
My words are clumsy stumbles;
Heard only by me...
Yielded to desperate mumbles.
-Words swallowed by the Sea.
When words are sequestered,
The sonnet shall be write.
Emotion shan't be sheltered.
Words dance in their plight.
To exchange words with another persona,
Is to dance under the eclipsed sun's corona.

## Sonnet No. 22

I must write a sonnet about Tapping-
Not simply to prove it works.
But to demonstrate I am more than yapping-
That these are educational quirks.
Like reading a map: endpoint in sight,
Stopping at the eye wall.
Turning 180. Fleeing in fright.
This method is uncomfortable for All.
Avoid dismissiveness before giving a chance.
The method is tried and true.
Experience will earn respect for the stance,
Without making the other'n blue.
If EFT's path makes you choke,
There are many other ways to get woke.

Zechariah N. Frame

# Sonnet No. 23

When the dances begin,
We both choose to lead.
Even when our steps are akin,
Both insist their own creed.
Each step, more force;
Each word, more proud.
A rigid dance marching a course
That begins attracting a crowd.
Lead is a title;
One who calls the shots.
But designation is not vital:
It's how we share our thoughts.
Dance. Always. Whether you lead or follow,
Otherwise, it's a solo. Merely leaving us hollow.

## Sonnet No. 24

One might think air time
Gets you closer to God.
Yet, it seems an earthly crime
For choosing the ground to trod.
The present is a gift.
For which we don't have to wait.
And through circumstance we sift;
Already at the Pearly Gate.
No. Air time allows me to ponder it all
-The only place far enough away
To make my maladies seem small...
...to keep the Demons at bay.
There is more to me than my circumstances show,
There's more to me than anyone can know.

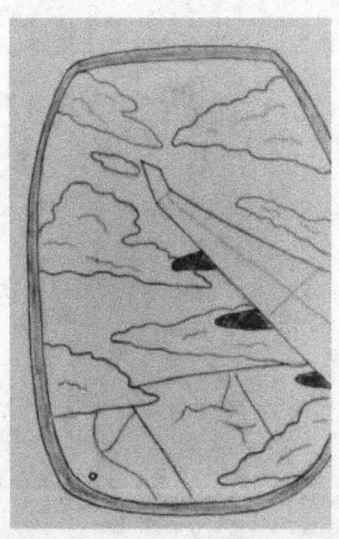

Zechariah N. Frame

## Sonnet No. 25

My view is low,
And of limited perspective.
I often wish it weren't so,
And was one I had selected.
When I find myself stuck,
As I now often do,
I question my luck,
In prolonged states of blue.
It could be heat, stress, or cold;
They all threaten longevity.
Take meds. Man up. Be brave, I'm told.
Excuses are mere scapegoats for Gravity.
Most days I long to be above the low floor.
But every day I resent Gravity a bit more.

## Sonnet No. 26

When my dude goes to the gym,
I know he goes for me.
I mean, really, I know he goes for him,
And we both like what we see.
Push-ups, benches, lats and rows...
They're all needed for upper body.
But he's been working head to toes,
Even though he's already a hottie.
And the best part of all,
Is not even physical;
It's how it makes him stand tall—
The reaction is truly chemical.
Always soak up good vibes like sponges.
Always remember to do those lunges.

Zechariah N. Frame

## Sonnet No. 27

It's that time of year:
When the sun comes around-
When balding is a fear-
Life circumstances abound-
Another year of experience-
And eight barrels of coffee-
Caff or decaf? Still on the fence.
Either would be good with toffee.
I hope this next lap around the sun
Will bring happiness in every way.
I'm so glad to know that I have The One.
This is a wordy way to say happy birthday!
Your gift doesn't come with an edible part,
This is a sonnet that comes from the heart.

## Sonnet No. 28

At the start, you thought you had 'em,
A marriage granted immunity.
The outcome is not what you fathom.
Missing is the sense of community.
Introducing new passion: an energy to nosh.
Adventures and Movement: granting a self wish.
Yet an overwhelming feeling still comes awash.
Shortcomings manifest as a rule to be selfish.
Your reflection is here, and has not turned his back.
Until you turn away.
But when you feel a lonely lack-attack,
There will certainly be lots to say.
The energy missing doesn't come from the Blue.
The energy missing is energy from you.

Zechariah N. Frame

## Sonnet No. 29

Don't lock me out of Heaven.
Please, it's Friday.
The hour is not even seven.
The night is still young, anyway.
Mario on the Switch...
I Feel Bad to Manifest...
Fun without a hitch.
You can decide which is best.
Thank you for Thai,
And buying a van.
Please let out a sigh.
Come be my man.
We don't have to be blue,
When it's just us two.

## Sonnet No. 30

When I let in the cold,
The shiver invokes a fear
that Mother never told
me would appear.
If I embrace the snow,
It will fall, and fall, and fall.
After I am buried, I will know
when I should have made the call.
After I break the trend
of manifesting snow and ice,
I find the most impactful way to mend,
Is by simply being nice.
The cold brings on a kind of anxiety;
The kind that often comes with society.

Zechariah N. Frame

## Sonnet No. 31

A friendship is a yin and yang.
The kind of story that
dances. -Despite the pang
of being bitten by a bat.
Friendship is an ebb and flow.
The kind of energy that passes
like time. We can't know
the last time we walk these grasses.
Friendships are always a history.
The kind that is written
in wood. A texture that leaves blistery
welts as if the grain had bitten.
But when a friend refuses to talk,
That's when friends learn to walk.

## Sonnet No. 32

At the request of my Best,
I am obliged to write a sonnet.
She is 1,000,000 miles West,
But my mind? She is on it.
I want to travel on her shoulder.
Because her pockets are too dark
to see the emotional boulders
she might think are stuck in park.
To my best friend that I love dearly-
I dream of going places with boom.
I want to travel to her tri-yearly.
And stow away in her hotel room.
Together always, but not like a creeper.
Just efficient. 'Cause she's a keeper.

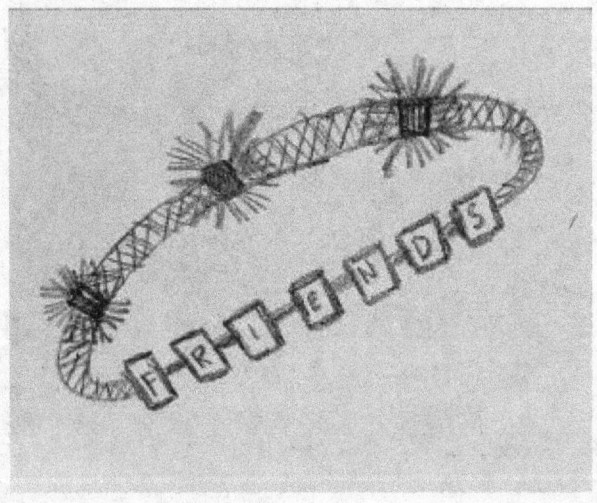

Zechariah N. Frame

# Sonnet No. 33

When we first met, I didn't think you were a mess:
Inked teardrop and bearded. But with honest eyes.
And on our first meeting, you were compelled to confess
the tortured truths from which you still rise.
Life is always teaching
us the lessons we need to grow.
Which is why we must keep reaching
for the knowledge we need to know.
So when Life's Lessons are being taught,
And you don't feel strong enough,
Know that your Spirit can't be bought-
Your experiences have made you tough.
Maybe it's from a past life I knew...
... never give up. I believe in you.

# Sonnet No. 34

When our skin meets,
I feel an intense
passion that heats
the heart in the best sense.
When our story is shared,
we both learn to show
how each other has cared-
Even if learning is slow.
When our paths diverge,
I often feel like a piece of my soul
has taken to a purge-
just trying to keep things whole.
As you sleep so soundly next to me,
I ponder a poisoned polyamory fantasy.

Zechariah N. Frame

## Sonnet No. 35

What about a past life?
A life of of prosperity and fame,
A life of peace or strife:
A life certainly not the same.
What lessons ought I learn?
Correcting errors from past life times
is daunting. But the soul will yearn
to understand the karmic crimes.
I choose to sit in the front row.
Persistent and poignant are the lessons.
The knowledgeable punch packs a blow
that sees us through our transgressions.
The lessons through lives we've had to whether,
Have taught us we're strong when we run together.

## Sonnet No. 36

It's not until you sleep
That I notice your settled mind.
For your waking mind seeks to weep
Rather than choose to unwind.
For most of us, gone are yesterday's pasts;
We learn our lessons and grow.
But your past pain presently lasts—
—Escape in substance so no one will know.
The fear! Filth. Guilt and shame:
The essential emotions to hide.
The lives you touch will never be the same.
The person you're hiding from lives inside.
I don't think our future has much hope,
If substance abuse is the only way to cope.

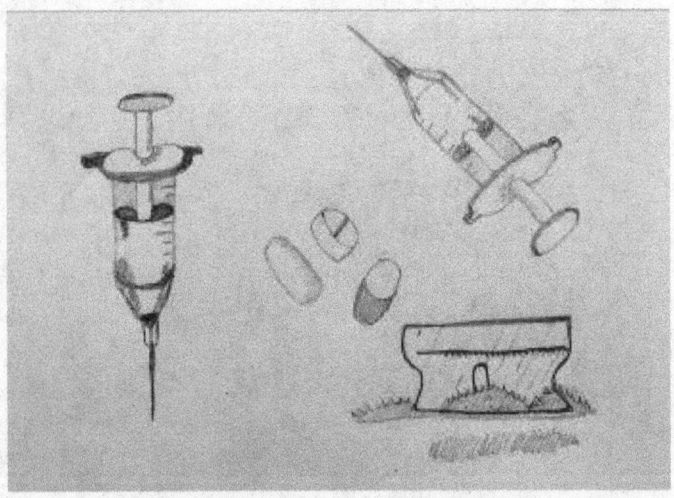

Zechariah N. Frame

# Sonnet No. 37

The moment was chill when he
returned from the Sheetz store.
He brought something for me
that usually leaves me wanting more.
Knowing my hubs is not a fan of drugs,
We assumed that's nicotine, too.
but when you're friends with former thugs,
You're always looking for something new.
The can was tossed casually at my feet,
My partner turned up his brow.
I was excited for an unexpected treat,
But my dude was going to let me have it now.
No, my dear, he did not buy me snuff,
It's a can of beef jerky: dried meat and stuff.

## Sonnet No. 38

The day we broke and learned we'd broken
Were not the same for us.
The lessons rest, waited to be woken-
Living from different views; not making fuss.
I broke over a ring of meaning.
You broke over a shattered West.
We broke. But we kept convening.
And we always give it our best.
What is gone is pruned and clipped-
to refocus the energy growing.
If we choose to beat or be whipped,
It's our dark colors we are showing.
Being broken was not our end.
It was a lesson in learning to bend.

Zechariah N. Frame

# Sonnet No. 39

Some days we want to waste in a hole
as a means to escape the Life unfolding.
-A hole to solidify what's missing in our soul.
-A hole that is appropriate for soul-holding.
It's human to want to retreat
to a cave of dirt, dank, and musk.
Especially when life's inconsistent beat
discards us like a shelled husk.
But if a hole is what they crave,
Choose one wide and spacious.
Step into the Sun, for its light will save
us when we can't be gracious.
Life can push us to become a hater,
But gravity is less in the Moon's crater.

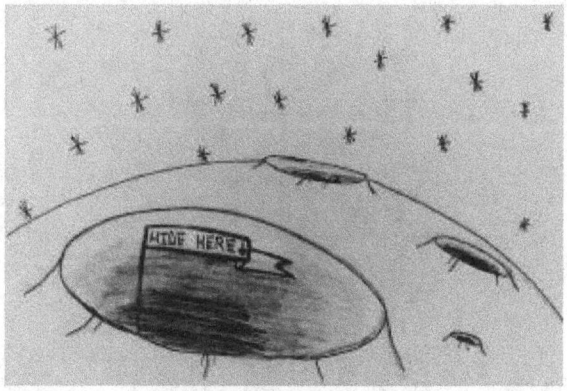

## Sonnet No. 40

Let's talk about the ways we communicate.
Our first fight was over Tupperware.
The worst part -and this is something I hate;
Is that the dialog was not even there.
Had you been cross-eyed fried,
You might had been more patient.
Instead of ensuring my dishes died
And making the anger so blatant.
Meth makes it hard to live life sober-
Especially when joy-receptors burned out.
But with help, you can learn to turn over
A new leaf and begin to shift your doubt.
Medical marijuana is good for your brain,
Yet it still takes a team to process the pain.

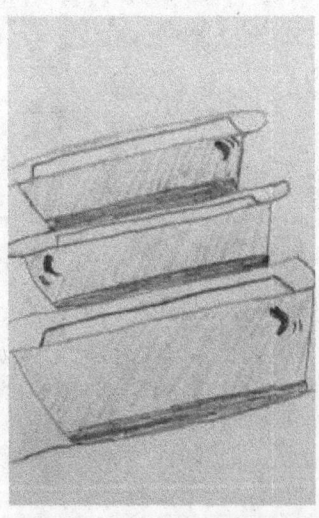

Zechariah N. Frame

## Sonnet No. 41

It was the summer of 2018,
As I was taking Charles for a walk.
I ran into a man who looked kind of mean,
but also attractive, so I stopped to talk.
He admitted to me he had done some times,
Which should have been a clue for me.
He clarified they were non-violent crimes.
I could look up his record, if I wanted to see.
This man reminded me of my rough roots,
The ones I pruned to survive.
And in that likeness, I shed his boots
So I may continue to grow and thrive.
Undoubtedly, we met for a good reason
But the circumstances say only this season.

## Sonnet No. 42

The earth shakes as my legs quake
violently as I try to sleep.
My neurology is the cause, Goodness sake.
To process the stress, I must weep.
To function I must climb a mountain fast:
A mountain that I must drive.
Some days, I don't think I can last.
Or try. Let alone survive.
Breathe. Stay calm. I'm not becoming stone.
I'm hot. And stressed. Exacerbating issues.
But there is fear, and panic. Don't leave me alone.
I can't cry anymore. I'm out of tissues.
To anyone else, they'd think I'm in psychosis.
But this is just another day with multiple sclerosis.

Zechariah N. Frame

# Sonnet No. 43

I want to tell about a group I'm in.
They are a fantastic family of folk.
Christians tend to dismiss them as sin.
(-and rebrand their holidays as a poke).
Our group meets for coffee every few weeks,
And we talk about metaphysical stuff.
We learn about the things our Spirit seeks.
We learn what makes each of us tough.
It's a group of greatness guided by love,
And consistently let the love be shone.
Even in the coffee line. They don't shove.
We no longer feel completely alone.
I'm thankful this group has motive to rally:
We are the Magickal Meetup of Teays Valley.

Savage Sonnets

# Sonnet No. 44

"Actions speak louder than words." She preaches;
As I again feel discarded and unconsidered.
She missed the lessons she allegedly teaches.
My heart, body, and mind feel littered.
It's easy to see flaws in relationships around us.
But when the time comes to step up and be,
It's easier to project, displace and fuss.
Coercing changes that best satisfy thee.
Waiting for the sign hasn't worked for us yet.
I don't have the energy to yell or shout.
I have passed my emotional threshold. Bet.
In the meantime, let's separate and pout.
I don't know what it is that I honestly wish,
On one side is love, the other side is selfish.

Zechariah N. Frame

## Sonnet No. 45

Daily, I wake with a renewed sense of panic;
What metabolistic quirk will misfire today?
I'm captain, but I won't go down with Titanic;
I'm sinking, taking on water in some way.
I must remind myself I've captured a bug-
Though I feel bitten by a venomous snake.
I'm reaching for the lifeline to give it a tug.
Even with help, the terror, I can't shake.
I'm chilled, yet my flesh burns to the touch.
I'm hot, yet too weak to disrobe.
I'm weak, yet my heart craves to do much.
I'm sick, I've been attacked by a microbe.
MS is scary even if you're a nonbeliever.
But terror ensues fast when you have a fever.

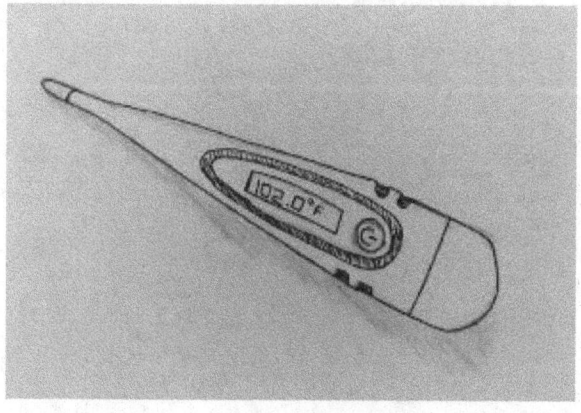

## Sonnet No. 46

When the sun rises on the dock,
I'm reminded the early time of day.
...loading, moving, and unpacking stock...
On a dock too far from the bay.
When the sun's in the sky about noon-high,
The 9-5er's take their rest.
But the task at hand begs asking "Why?"
The others can't be doing their best.
As the sun silently settles on the horizon,
I might get to catch it- but probably not.
By the time the sun sets, the day's forgotten.
... everything decanted to one tiny spot.
I yearn to know the position of the sun
that inspires life and the freedom to run.

Zechariah N. Frame

# Sonnet No. 47

In the life of the MSer,
Happenings are always booming.
Likewise, there's often a new stressor:
...today's started with shower and grooming.
Feeling brave, I unbuckled my seatbelt.
Started my trimmers and went to town.
After a few brief moments, a spasm I felt;
Though I resisted Gravity, I still fell down...
—Into the dog's water bowl, no less.
Naked, spastic, sad and wet,
I was feeling embarrassed, I confess.
Because I still had not manscaped yet.
MS really puts a guy into a funk,
When he loses the ability to trim his own junk.

## Sonnet No. 48

I can change my beard but not my MS.
My ensuing anxiety makes it hard to deal.
When I lose control and my best is far less,
I recognize my reality; the struggle is real.
Then I hear a voice; a strong support, smart.
I'm advised to THINK; take consideration.
The Inspiring bit we all ought take to Heart.
For every moment is a passing situation.
I reach to RISE knowing *I'm* what I got,
The thirst to thrive throws me to movement.
This is my life and I only got one shot,
And even a small victory is still improvement.
Even when the struggles and fears beget,
Forging the first steps begin with mindset.

Zechariah N. Frame

# Sonnet No. 49

In 2019, a virus emerged…
And it came from the east out of China.
The elderly, the sick and the weak -it purged,
"Wet markets!" -we believed them. Kinda.
The problem was bigger than locale of roots,
Stopping the spread was a bigger task.
The cure was not simply a gun that shoots.
It was one's willingness to wear a mask.
Millions have died; many still sick.
And it didn't have to be this way.
"We want it normal, bring it back quick!"
Like the virus, their selfishness will stay.
Contaminated air, breathing in spit broth;
Can be mitigated if we wear the face cloth.

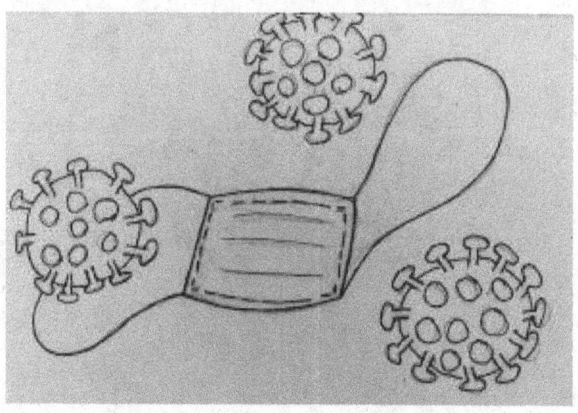

## Sonnet No. 50

At times during the day
I often crave snacks.
There's not much to say;
I'll eat snacks by the stacks.
And I'm not particularly particular
About the snacks I choose.
Though my selection can be curricular,
I have nothing to lose.
I like the snacks with crunch,
With fruit and sweet and chew.
Flavors dancing on the tongue so much;
I'll eat anything, between me and you.
"Eat your vegetables, open up, try it."
A lofty lifestyle change tends to outlast diet.

Zechariah N. Frame

## Sonnet No. 51

I have been begging for help for years,
My partner has done it all.
The sacrifice, the trauma, and the tears…
The tears that he never lets fall.
Purgatory-fashioned, autoimmune afflicted.
What did I do in a past life?
Constant dependence on which I'm addicted
Is the inherent source of my strife.
I yearn to be
in a place where
my body is free
and I don't need care.
One would think after all of this time,
I'd let go of thinking my disability is a crime.

## Sonnet No. 52

Happy anniversary to the man in my life,
Without you, I don't know where I'd be…
Maybe I'd be straight; try out a wife,
But that feels uncomfortable to me.
Our obstacles are plenty, and yet we survive,
We have seen more than the rest.
Even if the world gets hard -you and I thrive.
Because we both always give our best.
And maybe our moons inflame each other,
Our earth can keep us tame.
The truth is there isn't another,
Who could spoil me just the same.
15 years as my friend, partner and lover
Have given us a foundation of Love to cover.

Zechariah N. Frame

## Sonnet No. 53

When life is tough and you must shove,
To manage the "day to day-"
Reach into your pocket, pull out some love,
And smile. I have more to say:
Your love means more than all the wealth,
But a good diet is still key.
So let's pull out some keys to health,
So our years are healthy to be.
Anniversaries are more than a ploy-
It's a reminder to check our reflection.
Check, too, prominent pockets for joy,
As they offer life's sweetest confection.
15 years has definitely had hurdles,
But we swim on like a pair of sea turtles.

## Sonnet No. 54

Night and day I do my best
Or at least I think I do.
When you can't trust the rest,
I am there to console you.
From Snapchat to text,
Expressing love beyond streaks.
Evolving to feel emotionally hexed,
Laying low in the valley between peaks.
Unless I visit on your turf,
Some things won't be considered.
Exceptions, exceptions; I'll continue to surf.
Damned to feel ever-triggered.
… Amid our friendship, I feel used.
… Taken for granted and lightly abused.

Zechariah N. Frame

# Sonnet No. 55

Why Alaska (Peru) over other destinations-
When the bucket list is long?
It's a subconscious cause: I hate limitations.
-And want to feel free. Is that so wrong?
Niagara, New England, N'Orleans; and more,
Museums, and cruises, and shows.
Limitless things, right out the back door,
We should torch our travelor's woes.
This mouse isn't hungry for cookies, per se.
He is fatally famished for the impossible.
He will gnaw and chew away each day,
-Convinced, with planning, it *IS* possible.
Anywhere we go, we must be prepared.
And with flexible minds, we won't be scared.

## Sonnet No. 56

Now I feel alone, yet again.
And this is not a new feeling.
Rinsed and discarded for another man-
Can a calloused psyche speed healing?
Is it in my head? Am I just too sensitive?
Superior complexities explain it away.
Saying time is not there- that's pensative.
I'm consistently ignored day by day.
Sharing my life is starting to feel one-sided.
Time shows this is merely repeating history.
Ignoring all to find a love to confide in.
Canned responses leave a sense of mystery.
    Now that you are loved beyond a word,
    Whatever I add feels word-shaped and absurd.

Zechariah N. Frame

# Sonnet No. 57

Insanely jealous of my good friend's man,
And not for the reasons one'd think.
Good hair, nice bod, (not much of a tan)…
Genes. Hard work. No, that doesn't stink.
But feeling 1-up'd, does have a certain smell,
That ripe old feeling: discarded.
Many other poems have stories to tell.
And by unresolved issues, I am bombarded.
His ability to move a mountain for her,
Is the thing that makes her go.
Healthy? Or emotional chauffeur?
If she drives, then she will know.
A version of me who is straight and able.
Something sustainable; something stable.

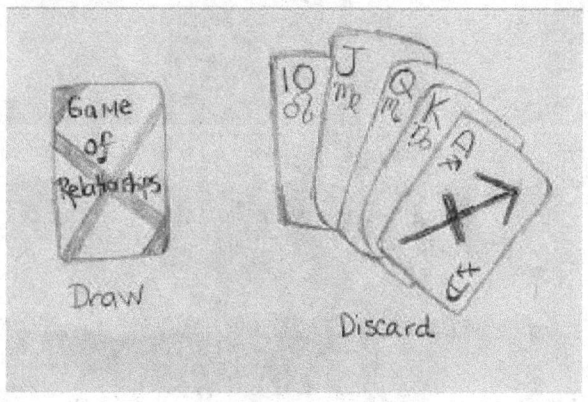

## Sonnet No. 58

I have nothing to say to you–
Words fail this time.
You wreck homes, indeed you do.
Stealing children is a crime.
Your trauma happened as young teen-
Losing the life of a new born.
Henceforth grief was begging to be seen
To heal the wound left torn.
Learning one's place is a lesson life-long,
You can't find it by kicking and crying.
Failing to cooperate is big time wrong.
And karma hits hard when you're lying.
When the trauma wounds are raw and revealing,
We should consider therapy to assist the healing.

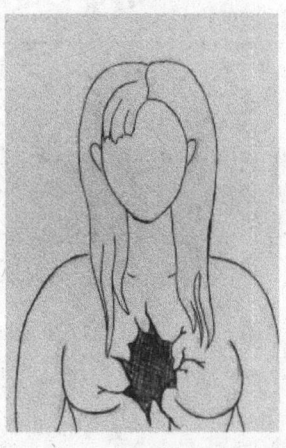

Zechariah N. Frame

# Sonnet No. 59

Children are a joy.
-At least when they aren't mine.
It is otherwise a ploy
To completely deplete all time.
Children are cute.
-From the other side of the room.
It's like the voices are mute,
…and I'm free to assume.
Children are miracles.
-When they are asleep.
That's when we consult our oracles-
And perhaps even think deep.
It's true, for some, children are their destiny,
But truthfully, I see, children are not for me.

## Sonnet No. 60

People do the number one
Inherently throughout the day.
Seldom is it a source of fun;
Suddenly sneaking away.
Panic ensues when I feel the urge
And I wonder where I can go.
Now time is limited; Bladder will purge.
I need to release and let it flow.
Can I hold it in time? Or blowout the dam?
Solving the stress with sadness and mess.
Ugly frustration is part of the scam
Cause sometimes it's fake MS.
Killing my soul via bladder bit by bit
Seems a simple target with a lasting hit.

Zechariah N. Frame

## Sonnet No. 61

Crashing daily each mid-afternoon…
Hours of time lost.
Rolling with the tides of the moon,
Otherwise I can't manage the cost.
Naps are needed to simply survive.
I know that now, and only through time.
Cat naps and siestas- this is how I thrive.
For without them my energy is slime.
All this fatigue prevents a life well-led:
This energy tank is broken.
I want to drive the farthest, without dread.
Going fast and flying free- I have spoken.
Under the surface, I'm still not free;
Enough are the days of Chronic Fatigue.

## Sonnet No. 62

Expectations of me that I had for Young Self
Are dreams shattered by disappointment.
In this life- my dreams are put on a shelf
For this affliction shows no adjournment.
Watching the world pass me fast by
In all of the aspects of life,
Leaves the incessant wondering "Why?"
Why is life daggered with strife?
Promotions, gatherings and freedom to run,
Are things for which I still grieve.
I want to be free and choose my own fun,
-Not frozen in mode of bereave.
Life's not fair when your partner is disabled.
For every aspect the Abled's life is tabled.

Zechariah N. Frame

## Sonnet No. 63

On one hand it's flattering
On how you think I believe.
On the other hand it's tattering
Believing a lie to deceive.
Sometimes I pray to God.
And sometimes I wish on stars.
Sometimes I notice the alignment of Yod.
I call on it All to heal my scars.
Like an honest child of the sky
I hope my thoughts to be heard;
I rest believing that Good is not shy;
But oft' a higher outcome is preferred.
Believing in stars doesn't make me delusional,
But it can if the beliefs become constitutional.

## Sonnet No. 64

When is it enough?
The battle has me worn.
I've proven I'm tough.
Yet old scars are torn.
Not giving up as we march on
And choosing to persevere,
Is a noble lesson we teach our spawn
When learning to challenge our fear.
But when in the war is there not enough wit?
When do we choose to flee?
When is it fair to fold and forfeit?
When can I finally rescue me?
The war with my body is never at rest,
So maintaining me is the least of my best.

Zechariah N. Frame

## Sonnet No. 65

What does it mean to have vision?
It's more than a physical sense.
It's the ability to make a decision;
Truth and Goodness are the best defense.
Let's be real, depth perception is nice,
We can appreciate proximity.
But left eye blind, adds fire to spice,
I lack affinity for vicinity.
Though I can't see the objects before me,
With vigor and depth and clarity-
I've been gifted with a talent to See.
And it's impact made up for this disparity.
The struggles are many when 1-eye blind,
Yet the gifts that make up for it are 1-of-a-kind.

## Sonnet No. 66

People make everything a prepared court case:
Even right to the bolts and nuts.
Often, it doesn't matter if they touch base;
Plainly kneading arguments that don't make cuts.
Late researchers know, all is on the Internet-
Exhausted with facts, many unfounded.
"Send regards." —with a loaded bayonet.
Consenting the wrong data to feel grounded.
Often we repeat our trauma,
Underestimating what is best.
Rallying behind life's drama
Then forsaking all the rest.
    If an abusive childhood inspires what we say.
    Then abusive parenting looks the same way.

Zechariah N. Frame

## Sonnet No. 67

We all need help when we first start out,
Of course, it's human to crave support.
Understand, there's no need to shout,
Honor goes far; reach to your cohort.
It's one thing to humbly ask for care
It's another thing just to expect it.
Especially when you act like a bear,
Lacking respect just to demand it.
You bleed the wallets of those you know,
No Fucks with all the entitled 'tude.
Taking advantage of those you "love;" Also,
Smiling doesn't make it less rude.
Leeches will suck the life out of you,
-Any chance proves, it's what you do, too.

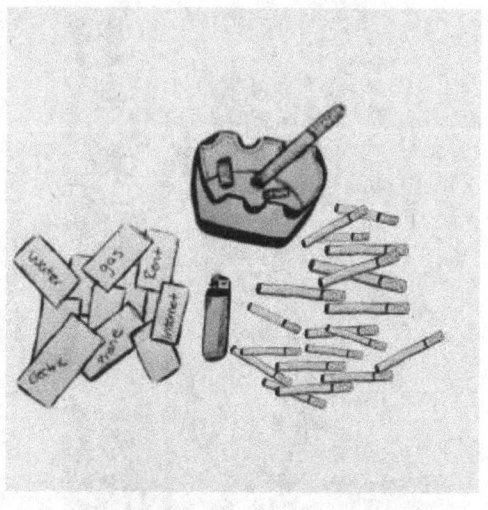

## Sonnet No. 68

Tall and protected is Rapunzel's tower
With basic needs, amenities and more.
Of course she's comfy, but has no power-
Girls behave and are not free to explore.
Afflicted internally within the high walls
Siblings compete to be seen.
Lingering resentment haunting the halls
Inspiring my soul to burn clean.
God sees all and knows my heart is pure;
Hellish emotions are my daily struggle.
The narcissism is thick, that is for sure,
Except, there's only two to juggle.
Right now I don't know when it'll be through
Since this is just life with Windy and Woo.

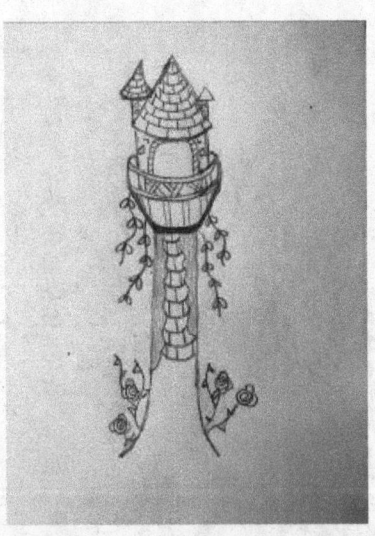

Zechariah N. Frame

# Sonnet No. 69

You showed up in my life in 2003,
On terms I had no choice.
Understanding why Mom wrecked the Christmas tree-
However, still not having much voice.
Out with the affair and with a married man!
My mother was broken and devastated.
Expecting to do more than I really can
We got used to you, but I always hesitated.
Resolving to abduct my younger sibling kids:
Ever far away, far from my mom and me.
Canceling plans and making other bids,
Keeping the truth masked so no one can see.
Even if I don't see you every day
Rightfully I find there is less and less to say.

# Sonnet No. 70

In my younger days, I had more ways,
To show up and be a good friend.
But now there's haze, and heavy it weighs,
There's a lack of energy to spend.
So what? I'm slow! There's still a soul in here.
Perhaps others have plainly forgotten.
We still need each other for sustainable cheer.
Or the forgotten fallen fruit will turn rotten.
I miss my friends and going out,
But my wheelchair wheels bring anxiety.
My bladder, and nerves and fear bring doubt,
Disability doesn't thrive in society.
Relationships fade out and slowly dissipate
When one, or both, simply don't communicate.

Zechariah N. Frame

# Sonnet No. 71

In this collection we have found joy and pain,
Disregard, replacement, pride, and fear.
And through the expression there was gain,
Facing the emotion makes it seem not near.
Five years or so is what we have uncovered,
Each poem has a full novel to tell.
Through writing, we hope the Self recovered;
Emotions that are free, don't typically dwell.
So cheers to the lessons I needed to grow,
Salud, to the other ones, too.
For now I have a record to show,
The progress I've made when I'm blue.
While the pain and suffering are never done,
I think this sonnet will conclude volume one.

# AFTERTHOUGHT

When I started this collection of poems five or so years ago, it was a private diary of my processed feelings. It was a sudoku for my emotions. I'm always seeking innovative solutions to my problems. And for these problems—these feelings—poetry was the answer.

Unfortunately, for me, some emotions are harder to process through poetry than others. Even today, I continue to process the lasting grief from losing my grandmother and my mother within four months of each other in 2014- and I am still learning how to process those emotions. We never get over the loss of a loved one, but through time, we learn to celebrate their memory. And that is what I would like to do here.

My grandmother had a pretty significant influence on my life growing up as my mom was a teen during her pregnancy. It's fascinating to me to learn that my grandmother dealt with many of her emotions through writing in the same way that I do. I wanted to remember and honor my grandmother by sharing a simple poem of hers that I found in a box of her writing after she passed.

Poetry captures a feeling or moment in time. "Now and Then" is a simple poem that acknowledges and appreciates being present in the moment. It is a

## Zechariah N. Frame

poem of being. It's acknowledging that there is beauty in everything, even through the passage of time.

The same can be said for the timelessness of these sonnets. They capture the moment in time, but even now, as I reread the poems, the meanings have shifted and changed. Angry poems are still beautiful, but different… And sometimes, even a little sour.

Savage Sonnets

## "Now and Then"

Some might say
    That the day
Is cloudy and gray.

    Snowy and cold it is
    But it keeps the pests away.

It brings joy to me
    When I see
That a tree can be

    Beautiful no matter
    Which season it may be.

Now I know
    That even tho
We grow and grow

    Especially when we're young
    Things are always too slow.

I've watched for hours
    How the flowers
Love the showers

    Then bloom and die.
    But vinegar always sours.

By Mary Frame 1985

## Zechariah N. Frame

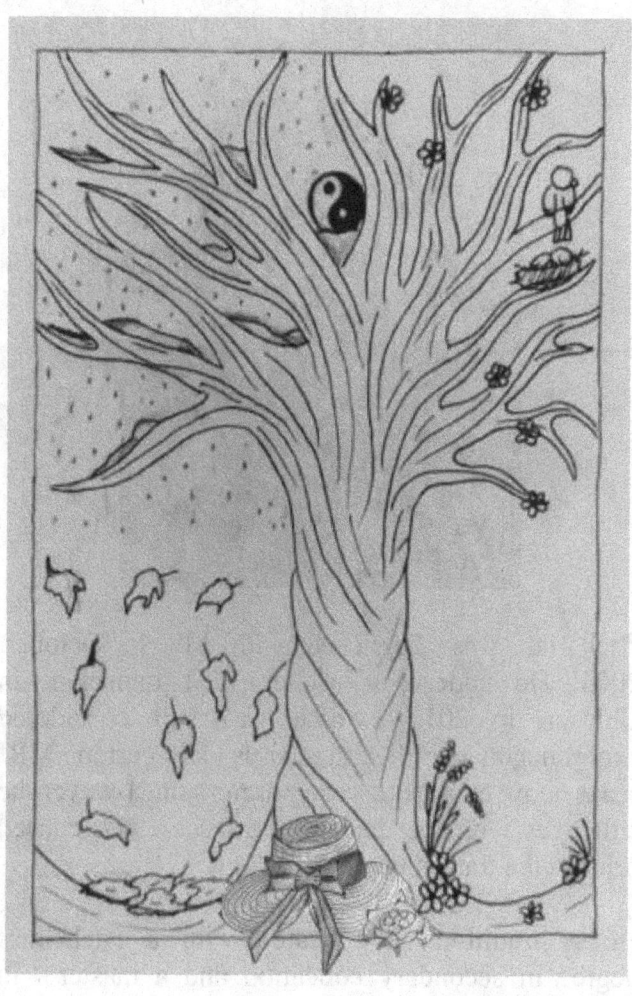

Zechariah was diagnosed with MS in October, 2005. He underwent a stem cell transplant in Chicago in 2017– which was still considered experimental by FDA standards. His current MRI scans show no new disease progression however, he still lives with the damage the disease has caused prior to the transplant.

He is traditionally educated with a bachelor's degree in secondary education and a master's in English from Marshall University. He has worked as an English as a second language teacher, a middle school speech teacher, and high school English and public speaking teacher. He also holds

## Zechariah N. Frame

a PhD in spiritual counseling and life coaching from the Institute of Metaphysical Humanistic Science. Currently, he works as a life coach, tarot card reader, and astrologer.

He lives with his partner in Hurricane, West Virginia with his cats, Allie and Evo, and his dog, Charlie.

## Savage Sonnets